This Book Belongs

To

....

....

TITLE

DATE

TITLE

DATE

TITLE

DATE

TITLE

DATE

TITLE

DATE

TITLE

DATE

TITLE

DATE

TITLE

DATE

TITLE

DATE

TITLE

DATE

TITLE

DATE

TITLE

DATE

TITLE

DATE

TITLE

DATE

TITLE

DATE

TITLE

DATE

TITLE

DATE

TITLE

DATE

TITLE

DATE

TITLE

DATE

TITLE

DATE

TITLE

DATE

TITLE

DATE

TITLE

DATE

TITLE

DATE

TITLE

DATE

TITLE

DATE

TITLE

DATE

TITLE

DATE

TITLE

DATE

TITLE

DATE

TITLE

DATE

TITLE

DATE

TITLE

DATE

TITLE

DATE

TITLE

DATE

TITLE

DATE

TITLE

DATE

TITLE

DATE

TITLE

DATE

TITLE

DATE

TITLE

DATE

TITLE

DATE

TITLE

DATE

TITLE

DATE

TITLE

DATE

TITLE

DATE

TITLE

DATE

TITLE

DATE

TITLE

DATE

TITLE

DATE

TITLE

DATE

TITLE

DATE

TITLE

DATE

TITLE

DATE

TITLE

DATE

TITLE

DATE

TITLE

DATE

TITLE

DATE

TITLE

DATE

TITLE

DATE

TITLE

DATE

TITLE

DATE

TITLE

DATE

TITLE

DATE

TITLE

DATE

TITLE

DATE

TITLE

DATE

TITLE

DATE

TITLE

DATE

TITLE

DATE

TITLE

DATE

TITLE

DATE

TITLE

DATE

TITLE

DATE

TITLE

DATE

TITLE

DATE

TITLE

DATE

TITLE

DATE

TITLE

DATE

TITLE

DATE

TITLE

DATE

TITLE

DATE

TITLE

DATE

TITLE

DATE

TITLE

DATE

TITLE

DATE

TITLE

DATE

TITLE

DATE

TITLE

DATE

TITLE

DATE

TITLE

DATE

TITLE

DATE

TITLE

DATE

TITLE

DATE

TITLE

DATE

TITLE

DATE

TITLE

DATE

TITLE

DATE

www.ingramcontent.com/pod-product-compliance
Lightning Source LLC
Chambersburg PA
CBHW070318240526
45467CB00046B/1420